# DEGAS

*Pastels*

by
Jacqueline and Maurice
Guillaud

Guillaud Editions Paris-New York
Clarkson N. Potter, Inc. New York

Guillaud Miniatures

# Degas and Pastel Painting

With his original use of pastels, Degas opened up new paths in modern painting. In the past, particularly in the eighteenth century, this medium had been exclusively a part of the draughtsman's repertoire, a means of adding color to drawings. Now it was raised to the "noble" rank of painting, thanks to the work of this enigmatic personality who stood alone on the fringes of Impressionism. It is significant that, while Degas' Impressionist col-

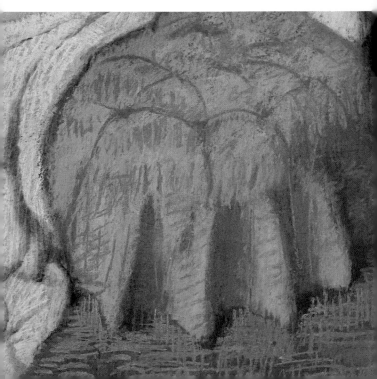

leagues took their easels out of doors, Degas worked in the shuttered intimacy of interiors.

Infusing his compositions with fragmented reflections of the light outside and harnessing it for his own means to glorify the subjects dear to his heart: women involved in the private rituals of daily life (in the bathroom) or earning their living (ballerinas); scenes of public life (the cafe, the opera, the music hall, the race course); scenes from the demi monde (the houses of ill repute); landscapes which Degas reconstructed, or amply invented. Over the course of many long years of productivity, Degas painted, traced and modeled all these pastels in multiple layers of blended colors. Sometimes he used pastel to color over the flowing monochrome lines of his expertly executed, superb and unique monotype prints. His development and perfection of this original mixed technique

heralded a new approach to painting; Picasso and other artists in subsequent generations, recognized the possibilities of this brilliant innovation. They studied and assimilated the lessons of this remarkable painter.

A Woman Having her Hair Combed, c. 1885
The Metropolitan Museum of Art (Bequest of Mrs. H. O. Havemeyer, 1929)

Front and back cover: After the Bath, c. 1885
Paris, Musée du Louvre, Cabinet des Dessins

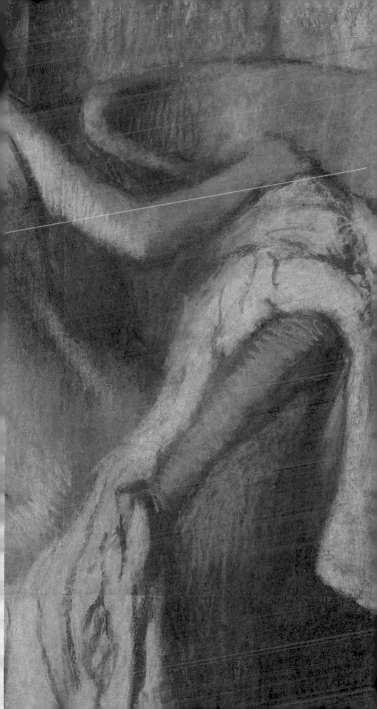

russet

drapes

russet

hair


russet light

on the

wall

with its

russet streaks

russet

strip

of rug


russet

shadow

on the

soft round

of the arm


on the gentle

hand

that lifts

the russet mane


in the small

of the back

on the firm

flesh

of the belly

After the Bath, 1888
London, The National Gallery

Woman Leaving the Bath
Paris, Musée du Louvre (Bequest of Victor Lyon)

Woman at her Toilette, c. 1903
The Art Institute of Chicago (M. and Mrs. M.A. Ryerson Collection)

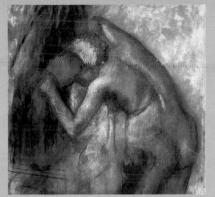

Woman Drying her Hair, c. 1900/1905
Lausanne, Musée Cantonal des Beaux Arts

After the Bath, Woman Drying her Chest, 1890
London, Courtauld Institute Galleries

The Tub, c. 1891
Glasgow, The Burrell Collection

the towel is
a fluffy
cloud
of spray

cascading

over
neck

and
throat

down

the back of
the chair
offered to
the woman
while intent,
she goes through
the motions of
drying

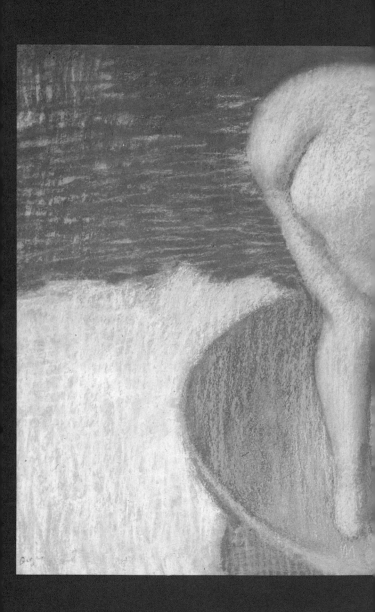

an expanse
of sea

flecked with
orange
oil-slicks

a skiff
skims
over the waves

round
flat-bottomed
tub
of zinc

silently
gliding on

leaving a
foamy
wake
behind

on
deck

a naked
body
bends
forward

the
coursing
blood
tinges
the skin

that
will not be
denied

carnal
stirrings
assail

the
toilette
as
rite
and sensual
fulfillment

Edgar Degas (1834-1917)

Degas was born into a middle-class family (his father was a banker) in Paris in 1834. He gave up the study of law at the age of 21 to enroll at the Academy of Fine Arts. An admirer of Ingres, he visited Italy from 1856 to 1857,

Woman Leaving her Bath, c. 1895/98
Switzerland, Kunstmuseum, Solothurn, Dübi-Müller

where he copied the works of the Renaissance masters. In 1858, Braquemond introduced him to the technique of engraving, and around this time he discovered Japanese prints, which would later inspire the spatial arrangement of his compositions. He did many drawings, and in 1860 painted members of the Italian branch of his family in *The Bellelli Family*, a large-scale portrait which now hangs in the Orsay Museum. Influenced by Ingres and Puvis de Chavannes, Degas was also attracted to historical subjects (*Misfortune of the*

The Tub, 1886
Paris, Musée du Louvre, Cabinet des Dessins

*City of Orleans*, 1865). His enthusiasm for the world of theatre and music is documented in such paintings as the bassoonist Dihaut in *The Orchestra of the Opera*. In 1872, Degas sailed to New Orleans, his mother's birthplace, to spend a few months with relatives. *The*

*Cotton Market.* On his return to France, he took part in the first exhibitions of the Impressionists (1874-79), though a number of fundamental differences set Degas apart from this group. Neither his own, nor his colleagues' paintings met with great success. A believer in realism and

The Tub, 1886
Farmington, Hill-Stead Museum

drawn to the literary current of naturalism, Degas painted many portraits and genre scenes (*Women Ironing, Absinthe, The Rape*). What he witnessed on visits to the theater, the opera and the circus, as well as his fascination with ballet-dancers and their milieu, provided him with abundant subject matter. Experimenting with monotype (a technique in which he soon developed an unequaled mastery) Degas portrayed evenings at the theatre and hostesses and clients in brothels. Women were his constant source of inspiration. Degas had a solitary character. His friends found him hard to get along with and as he grew older began to distance themselves from him. His isolation continued to increase and he was plagued by failing eyesight. At the end, he stopped painting altogether, and developed an innovative technique of pastel work. At the same time, he created a series of wax figures, notable for the astounding precision with which he captured the gestures and motions of dance. Only after the artist's death in 1917 were bronze casts made of these wax models, many of which, however, were in very poor condition.

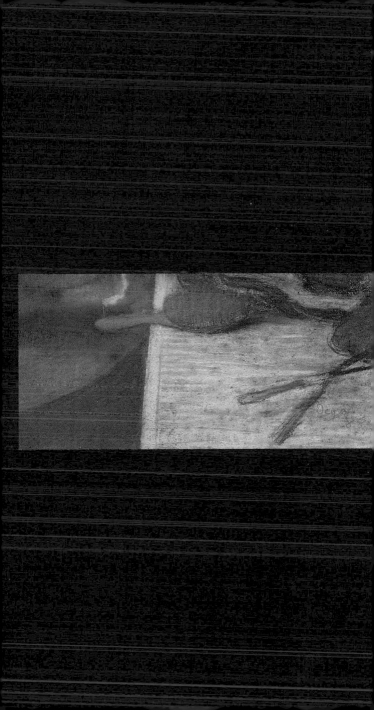

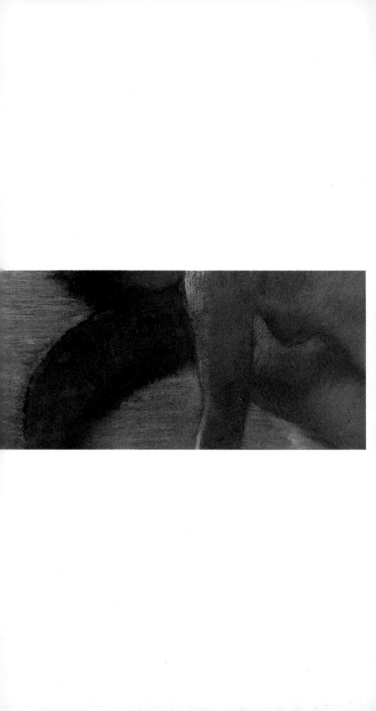

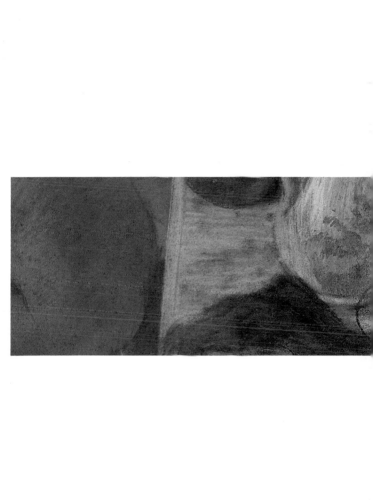

glints
of water
on the
surface
of
the
carpet

streaks
of
autumnal
light

patch
of
foam
lapping
linen-white
around
the
vessel

that
drifts

imperceptibly

bending
suppley
- though
the angle is
acute -

the woman
- the girl -
chastely
suffers
the attentive eye
to graze
her naked body

her hand
polishes
the deck of
the intimate
boat

sailing
as on a
voyage

the
redness
of her
hair

ripples
down
to
the hip
in its
faint
blue
shadow

the morning
sun
steals in
from the side,
muted

almost
cold

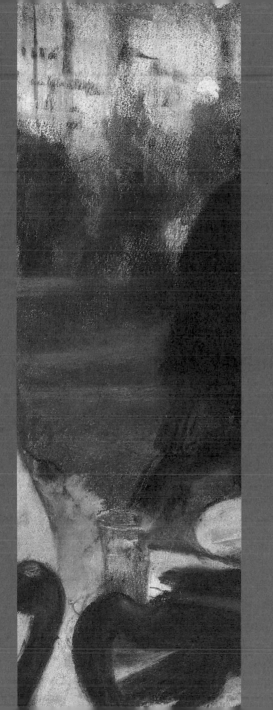

Women in Front of a Café, c. 1877
Paris, Musée du Louvre, Cabinet des Dessins

Mrs. Dietz-Monin, 1879
The Art Institute of Chicago (Joseph Winterbotham Collection)

At the Café-Concert, 1885
Paris, Musée du Louvre, Cabinet des Dessins

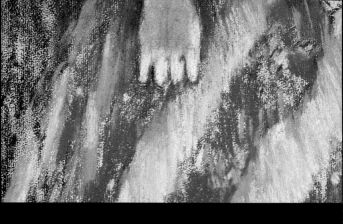

slender
rounded
hand
against the
bayadere taffeta

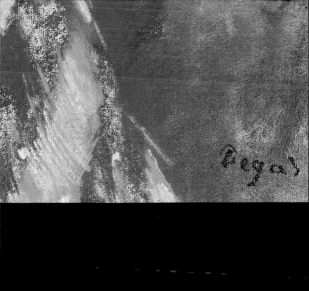

the song
takes
flight
and cuts through
the hubbub
of the
music-hall
where
the belles

repose

time stands still
for a moment
in this life of
breaking off
and

day after
day
rehearsing
anew
the postures
the sequences
the leaps

pause

respite

solitude

echos
of
exertions
and
resurgence
of
odors of gestures
practiced
to please

the
great hall
is
empty

yet
the floor
still
reverberates
from
the steps
called
by the
ballet-master

The Singer in Green, 1884
The Metropolitan Museum of Art (Bequest of Stephen C. Clark)

Dancers Resting, c. 1880
Boston, Museum of Fine Arts (Juliana Cheney Edwards Collection)

from
the
sticky
confines
of the
stage box

he trains
his glass
on
the line
of legs
of the
quadrille

glimpses
of
pink
beneath
the blue tulle
of
the costumes
alive with
music

the vision
swirls
in the
orchestral
bacchanale
that
intoxicates
dancers and
audience

the
diva
swoons

eyes
closed
to the
dancing
flare
of
the
gas-lamps

Degas

L'Attente, c. 1882
J. Paul Getty Trust, Norton Simon Foundation

Dancer Adjusting her Slipper
Paris, Musée du Louvre, Cabinet des Dessins

Two Dancers, c. 1880
Leipzig, Museum für Geschichte der Stadt

Dancers in Violet, 1903
Switzerland, Private Collection

Dancer Bowing, c. 1877
Paris, Musée du Louvre

Dancers at the Old Opera House, c. 1877
The Art Institute of Chicago

like
an optical
puzzle,
one
strains
one's eyes
to decipher
the cliff

jutting out

into the sea.
Observe
the woman:
no sense of shame
beneath her
camouflage
she straddles
the promontory
that tapers away
into the distance
but
it is
a couch
the naked
body sprawls on
in the mild

coolness
of the afternoon
like a carpet
of flowers
in profusion
on the meadow
above
the blue
it takes

shape

legs drawn up
hair
tumbling down
the nipples
tremble
under the
slow caress
of a
gentle breeze

between the
fleshy thighs
shadow offsets
the pink
flowers
of the flank

a mountain

horizon

shelters

the privacy

of the glimpse

into the room,

wide open

to the

whiteness

of a new

present

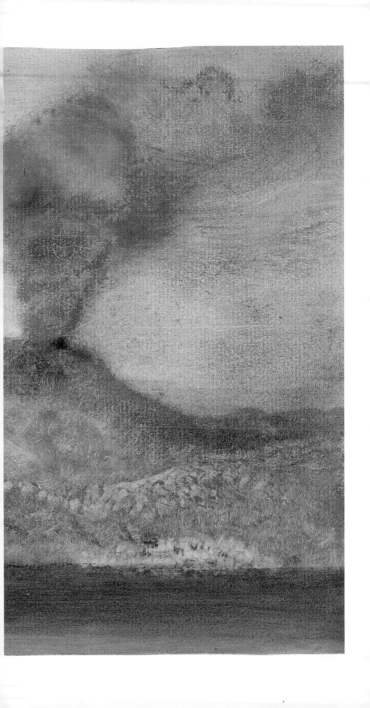

Mlle Dumay (singer), c. 1877/79
Cincinatti, John W. Warrington

Landscape, c. 1892
Genève, Galerie Jan Krugier

Vesuvius, 1890/92
Berne, E. W. Kornfeld

The 24 pastel reproductions
After the Bath (two details, front and back cover); A Woman
Having her Hair Combed (five details, overall 74 x 60,6); After
the Bath (overall 48 x 87); After the Bath (two details);
Woman Leaving the Bath (two details); Woman at her Toilette
(two details); Woman Drying her Hair (detail); After the Bath
(overall 103,8 x 98,4); Woman Leaving the Bath (overall 70 x
70); Woman at her Toilette (overall 74,7 x 72,3); Woman
Drying her Hair (overall 77 x 75); After the Bath, Woman
Drying her Chest (overall 68 x 59); The Tub (overall 59 x 83);
After the Bath, Woman Drying her Chest (two details); The
Tub (two details); Woman Leaving her Bath (two details,
overall 94,5 x 80,5); The Tub (overall 60 x 83, three details);
The Tub (overall 70 x 70, six details); Women in Front of a
Café (three details, overall 41 x 60); Mrs. Dietz-Monin (two
details, overall 85 x 75); At the Café-Concert (overall 26,5 x
29,5, two details); The Singer in Green (three details); Dancers
Resting (five details); L'Attente (two details); Dancer Adjusting
her Slipper (detail); Two Dancers (two details); Dancers in
Violet (two details); The Singer in Green (overall 58,4 x 45,7);
Dancers Resting (overall 50 x 58,5); Dancers in Violet (detail);
Dancer Bowing (three details); Dancers at the Old Opera
House (two details); Mll Dumay (two details); L'Attente
(overall 47 x 60); Dancer Adjusting her Slipper (overall 62 x
49); Two Dancers (overall 98 x 89); Dancers in Violet
(overall); Dancer Bowing (overall 72 x 77,5); Dancers at the
Old Opera House (overall 22 x 17,2); Landscape (two details);
Vesuvius (two details); Mlle Dumay (overall); Landscape
(overall 42 x 55); Vesuvius (overall 25 x 30)
Measurements given in centimeters

Texts and design by Maurice Guillaud

© 1989 Jacqueline and Maurice Guillaud

Library of Congress Cataloging-in-Publication Data
Guillaud, Jacqueline and Maurice
Degas, pastels
1. Degas, Edgar, 1834-1917. I. Degas, Edgar. 1834-1917. II. Guillaud,
Maurice. III. Title.
NC248.D38A4 1989a 741. 944   88-32388
ISBN 0-517-573067

Published by Clarkson N. Potter Inc. , 225 Park Avenue South
New York NY 10003
Represented in Canada by the Canadian MANDA Group
Published in France by Guillaud Editions 70 rue René Boulanger 75010
Paris
Manufactured in Italy - Bound by S.P.B.R. France